# CREATING AN ONLINE

# INCOME STREAM

# CREATING AN ONLINE

# INCOME STREAM

By

## Elena Saris

2022
United States of America

# Table of Contents

# INTRODUCTION

Some of you reading this may be ready to escape your cubicle and leave your 9-5 job in the rear-view mirror forever. Others may just want to supplement their kid's college fund, buy a new car, or just have some extra money in the bank to give you peace of mind in these uncertain times. My goal is to help you understand the myriad of ways people are creating profits online and give you detailed information about these opportunities so you can understand *what it really takes to succeed.*

So many people think "Make Money Online" offers are a scam because they have been lied to for so long by hucksters peddling "Passive Income Opportunities." Online businesses are NOT passive income. They take work and dedication. However, once you build the foundation, much of the work can be automated or outsourced and you can earn a full-time income working 10-15 hours a week.

This book is not intended as an exhaustive list of the different ways people are creating and online income stream, but rather a detailed outline of the opportunities and an honest comparison of each.

Here is the bottom line: ALL online income streams require you to **create an offer:** goods or services that you create or someone else has created, **generate traffic to that offer:** get people to see the offer, and **build an email list:** get the email contact information of the people who would be inclined to purchase that offer. If you build a website and you put an item up for sale on that site but do nothing else, it will simply live on the world wide web in utter obscurity forever. The internet is not Field of Dreams, no one is coming. You must INVITE, ENTICE, or INFORM people about your offer.

Course after course and book after book will claim to teach you how to make "passive income" online. They will offer to help you build a site, or create a course, start a blog, but they fail to mention that this is just the easy first step. As someone who is dedicated to helping folks truly understand the online income opportunity, these claims are infuriating to me because they are misleading people about what it really takes. And sadly, this has caused thousands of people to give up hope because they did not understand the process. Making the offer is just step one, getting customers to see your offer is the key to success.

You must learn to drive traffic to your offer. Reputable courses will teach you this in great detail. People brand new to digital marketing can absolutely learn this skill. And once you do, you can create success in nearly any online platform.

There are different types of traffic you need to know about. A customer's journey to any offer involves three stages:

**Awareness, Evaluation, Conversion.** They need to know the thing exists (physical goods, services, digital E-books). They then consider whether they want to buy that thing and finally, they choose among offers of that thing and make their purchase. Driving traffic to the different stages of the customer journey takes different levels of effort, costs and methods. These will be explored in detail.

There are also several ways to find or create offers that you will drive traffic to. In the pages to come, you will hear the *straight truth* about what investment, in time and money, is required to make them work. You will see a full break down of how long it will take to make your first dollar, the degree of difficulty the average person will have in learning the platform, the potential income you can expect with success and the risk level involved.

It is my hope that as you learn about these platforms and strategies, one resonates with you and makes you want to explore the opportunity more. Working online requires only a computer and a reliable internet connection. Imagine living life on your own terms, working on your own schedule, taking a sick day without asking permission and catching your kid's weekday afternoon sports game without playing hooky.

One important note I want to emphasize is this: Tech skills are not required. If you can attach a picture to an email, you have the necessary skills. It's true that in the early years, it really did take tech know-how or even coding knowledge. In the past 10 years though, the advances in technology, new software and easy to use tools, have really opened up the online income opportunity to everyone.

I learned how to type on a manual typewriter, had an 8-track player in my first car and up until one year ago, had a working rotary phone as a landline. There is literally no excuse to delay getting in on this opportunity. Do not let the technology part of any of these platforms stop you.

The explanations of the opportunities I include in this book are not meant as a training or "how-to" but rather a "learn about what is out there." My rating scale speaks to the average person who wants to learn digital marketing. 90% of people who randomly buy a course to learn how to make money online, will abandon it when it seems too complicated or when they hit a roadblock.

The monthly income that I am forecasting here in my potential income chart focuses on what the *average successful* person makes. There will always be outliers, superstars who work 14-hour days or someone who happens to hit upon a viral trend. Those are the success stories most gurus use in their sales pitches, the top 1% of the 10% who find success. I sincerely hope that should you start on this journey, you become one of those. But going in, I want you to know how most folks who find success fare on the various platforms. And keep in mind, once you achieve a certain level of success, you can certainly grow and scale your business by adding more time, money, or resources.

This book does not need to be read in order. As you begin to explore certain platforms, if you decide right away that this is not the one for you, feel free to skip ahead to the next platform. Each platform description also contains a summary at the end of what it takes to be successful and a graph showing you the overall breakdown.

Let's Dive in…

The most common ways creating an online source of income fall into these 6 Categories:

## E-commerce:

Selling physical or digital goods online.

## Affiliate Marketing:

Earning a referral fee for selling other people's physical or digital goods online.

## Gig Work:

Selling your individual services to people online. Trading dollars for hours.

## Agency/Drop Servicing:

Creating a team of gig workers and reselling their services online.

## Books:

Writing or publishing other people's books in the Amazon Kindle Direct Press marketplace.

## Expert/Course Creator:

Getting paid to teach other people your specific skill set.

We will explore all of these, and I will give you a chart indicating the following for each platform:

**Degree of Difficulty:** How hard is for the average person to learn and implement this platform.

## Is the platform good for:

*Beginners:* Folks completely new to the online money-making space.

*Intermediate:* Folks who have tried some online income opportunity with varying levels of success.

*Advanced:* Folks who have already had success making money online.

**Upfront Costs:** How much money do you need to begin. This cost analysis assumes that you will be paying for at least some education and/or software on top of what is required.

$ Under $1,000

$$ $1,000-3,000

$$$ $3,000-5,000

$$$$ $5000-$10,000

$$$$$ Over $10,000

**Time to First Sale:** From when you go "live" how long will it be until you can expect at least one sale – noted in months. This means *revenue*, not profit.

**Potential Income:** Average *monthly profit* for a successful seller, not a "dabbler" and not a "superstar."

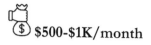 **$500-$1K/month**

**$1k-$5K/Month**

**$5K-$10K/month**

**Over $10K/Month**

**Generating Traffic to Your Offer:** How difficult will it be for you to get folks to see your offer. (Do not be dissuaded by a designation of high, with more effort generally comes more profit potential.)

## Effort level:

*Low*: Fairly easy. Generally, means the platform has a traffic source already and standing out is not terribly hard.

*Medium:* Takes a fair amount of work or money for ads. For traffic to close a sale, you must stand out in a crowd of interested buyers where others are also competing heavily to stand out. For traffic to bring awareness to an offer and have someone else close the sale, you must generate that on your own, but that is not as difficult as generating buyer traffic.

*High:* Takes a lot of work or money for ads. You must create awareness for your own offers generate all the buyer traffic on your own.

**Own Your Own Customers:** Will this platform leave you with an Email List you own or a following online?

## Likelihood:

*Low:* The platform is not set up for you to build your own customer list.

*Medium:* You can build a list with extra efforts, or you can build "followers" on a social media platform, but you must get their off-platform contact info yourself.

*High:* You build and own your list from the outset.

**Risk Factor:** What is the level of risk for you if you fail miserably. This mainly refers to monetary risk, not time spent.

# CHAPTER 1

---

# E-COMMERCE – SELLING PHYSICAL PRODUCTS ONLINE

When you think about it in general, any transaction you do online is "E-commerce." I use the term here to speak specifically of selling physical goods. You can sell physical goods on your own website, or you can be what's called a "3rd party seller" on sites like Amazon. Let's start with Amazon. There are 3 ways you can sell physical products on Amazon (we will discuss selling books separately). One is to "Private Label" a product, another is to buy an item from a wholesale distributor and resell it online and finally there is Merch, which is short for "merchandise" where you sell designs that will be placed on T-shirts and the like.

## AMAZON PRIVATE LABEL

Most people don't realize this but when you shop on Amazon, you are not always buying from Amazon. Approximately 65% of all transactions on the Amazon marketplace are between the customer and a 3rd party seller. That seller has sourced an item from a manufacturer, purchased inventory in bulk and sent it to one of many Amazon warehouses. They created a listing for that item on the Amazon marketplace and one of the Amazon warehouses will store that item until its purchased. Then Amazon will pack and ship that item to the customer who ordered it from your listing. For that service, you will pay a 15% commission and a "pick and pack" fee which varies depending on the size, shape and weight of the item.

Success in this venture involves choosing the right item which takes loads of research, purchasing software to show you back-end details of items already for sale on Amazon, and finding a manufacture of that item who can get it to you at a price low enough for you to turn a profit after Amazon's cut. Once you have the product chosen, you must then work on making sure your item appears at the top of the Amazon listing page when buyers come to the platform and type in the name of your item. You must get reviews to your item, so people feel safe in buying it from you. You must continually maintain inventory that you must buy in bulk upfront. You must advertise your item, either through ads on social media or ads on the Amazon platform to consistently be seen near the top of the page when buyers come to Amazon.

The benefit of selling on Amazon is that *all* of the people who come there are *buyers*. They are not looking at pictures of cats, or funny memes. They are not doing research. They are there to *buy* something, your job is to get your listing to be the thing they want to buy. When a buyer chooses your item, you get paid. Amazon stores and ships your item and handles customer service and returns. While this may seem like a good thing, keep in mind it is a double-edged sword. They do this because that buyer is their customer, not yours. You are not building an email list of eager buyers. There are some workaround ways with extra cost and time that can get you a portion of your customer's information, but the main way Amazon is set up, is for you to send traffic to their site so Amazon can obtain customers.

Amazon is a traffic source, not a business. You can build your business on their platform, but you are subject to platform and policy changes that you have no say in and cannot control. The potential for income is high but I would not recommend this to anyone who did not have $10-$15K at a minimum to spend upfront and 8-12 months before seeing a sale. Keep in mind, you must pay in advance for your inventory so there is also substantial risk if you chose the wrong item, and no one wants to buy it.

**In order to be successful in this endeavor, you must:**

- Choose the right product (one in high demand that can be sourced cheaply enough to turn a profit).
- Design the packaging or tweak the product so that it is unique to you in some way.
- Source the product from a manufacturer.
- Pay upfront for inventory and continually monitor inventory.
- Create a compelling listing for the product on the Amazon Marketplace.
- Get reviews for your item.
- Try to "rank you item" so that when people type in the relevant "keyword" your item shows up at the top of the first page.
- Continually drive traffic to your offer so that you don't lose ranking because of dwindling sales
- Continuously monitor inventory levels so that you always have inventory available in the Amazon warehouse to meet sales demand, but not too much so as to accrue excessive storage fees.

## Traffic Generation:

Awareness, Evaluation and Conversion: On Amazon, a customer is aware of the item they want to buy and it's the seller's job is to stand out in the evaluation stage, so they choose their offer over the other offers. The conversion is hassle free as Amazon has a good reputation and people do not think they will be scammed. You are not generating the traffic; you are convincing existing traffic in the evaluation stage to choose you.

# AMAZON
# PRIVATE LABEL

Degree of Difficulty to Learn

INT-ADV

Upfront Costs

$ $ $ $ $

Time to First Sale

**8M-12M**

Income Potential

$ $ $ $

How Hard to Drive Traffic

**Medium**

Builds Your Email List

**Low**

Risk Level

**High**

# AMAZON WHOLESALE

When we speak of "Amazon Wholesale" we are referring to a 3rd party Reseller who buys items from wholesale distributors and sells those items at retail on the Amazon marketplace. The goal is to buy the right items from a reputable wholesale distributor and sell them for more money than the purchase cost. Think of a local 711 store where you might go in to buy Colgate toothpaste. The 711 store didn't create the toothpaste. They contracted with a distributor of the toothpaste and were able to get it for a price that allows them to offer it for sale in their store and sell it for more than that price to make their profit. You can do the exact same thing online in the Amazon Marketplace.

Amazon has millions of product pages. Anyone can place an offer on most any product page. These are different than private label listings. You do not create a new offer though; you place your offer on an existing product page. If your offer is deemed "competitive" by Amazon, they will include you as a featured merchant in the "buy box" for a certain percentage of time. That may sound weird, but it means that when customers hit the "ADD TO CART" button they are going to get the same item each time, but the VENDOR of that item changes periodically. Resellers "share the buy box" so they get a percentage of the sales of that item each month. To be "competitive" in Amazon's eyes, your price and your delivery times must be roughly equivalent to the sellers currently selling that item.

As a very basic and simple example: If there are four competitive sellers on a listing for Colgate toothpaste and you learn that 100 units of toothpaste are sold per month, then on average each of those sellers is moving 25 units per month. If you are able to get on the listing, then each seller will move 20 units per month. Ideally you would only need to keep 30 days of inventory in stock at a time, however, when supply chains are tight due to extraordinary events, you can purchase up to 60 days of each product to prevent running out of stock prematurely. In this example your upfront investment, even assuming you need a 60-day supply, is 40 units. This is a much smaller investment than private label sellers who must order in bulk upfront and meet minimum order quantities of their unique products of 1000-5000 units at a time.

In order to be a successful seller, you will need to find suppliers who are looking for competitive sellers to whom to distribute. These sources are traditionally wholesale distribution companies who have purchased in bulk from numerous brands in order to resell in smaller quantities to retailers. You want to be one of those online retailers they work with. Your goal is to find suppliers who can deliver items to you at a price that allows you to make a profit on an item that has enough monthly sales to keep in your stable of products.

Normally the wholesale distributor will give you a spreadsheet file of everything they sell. This will include all the data you need to determine if that product is something you can resell successfully. You can manually review these files but there are different software options out there that will allow you to process spreadsheets quickly to determine which products can be purchased and resold at a profit.

This platform requires loads of research, but your upfront inventory costs can be quite small while you learn the system. This is a volume game, but one can grow as slowly or as quickly as your time and resources allow. Best of all, once you have mastered this platform on our own, nearly all of this can be outsourced to workers you hire who can do the research, list the items, maintain inventory levels and work with suppliers.

**In order to be successful in this endeavor, you must:**

- Find the right products that are selling consistently and without much competition from other sellers.
- Find a supplier who is willing to sell it to you at the right price and who has consistent inventory.
- Create your offers for each of these products and place them on the corresponding pre-existing Amazon listing.
- Purchase your initial inventory.
- Keep up to date on your inventory that you purchase in advance, making sure to stay in stock, but not accrue storage fees for items that stay in the warehouse too long.
- Continue to find more and more products so that you have hundreds if not thousands of offerings.

## Traffic Generation:

Awareness, Evaluation and Conversion: The listing is there already for you. You need not generate traffic, your work lies in the evaluation stage, but that is mainly between you and Amazon. If Amazon deems your listing to be competitive with other offers on the listing in terms of price, quality, and delivery time then Amazon will show your offer a certain percentage of the time and you will get the conversion.

# AMAZON
# <u>WHOLESALE</u>

Degree of Difficulty to Learn

Upfront Costs

Time to First Sale **1-2M**

Income Potential

How Hard to Drive Traffic

Low

Builds Your Email List

Low

Risk Level

Low

# MERCH BY AMAZON (MBA)

Merch is short for merchandise. You design or pay to have someone design, a picture or saying that can be printed on merchandise ranging from T-shirts to Cell Phone cases. The Amazon platform provides you with a page that has a mockup of a blank shirt or cell phone case. You upload your design onto that canvas and send traffic to that design. When a buyer selects your item, Amazon will print the item on demand, ship it to the customer for you and send you a royalty payment. This is also a volume game as you only earn a percentage of each sale. As an example, at the time of publication of this book, a T-shirt selling for $19.99 will earn the designer $5.21. A Phone case selling for $19.99 will earn the designer $4.28.

While Amazon is a great traffic source for items people know they want to buy, the competition is a bit different for these items as no one is typing in the exact words of your text design or the name of the picture you designed. Successful sellers will find passionate niches and create designs around those niches that fans will actually search for. For example, an avid gardener looking for a gift for a friend may type in "Funny gardening

T-shirts." Trends also can be monetized. One of the most successful single shirts I have heard of on the platform was a shirt commemorating the Solar Eclipse of 2017. So while there are many buyers, you must compete with sellers in the same niche to have them choose your shirt over all others.

Sellers must "tier up" in order to be allowed to list more and more items. Meaning you must sell a certain number of items before Amazon allows you to list move to the next tier. The tiers start at 10, 25, 100, 500, 1000 and it takes time to move up. The sellers I am personally familiar with who make over $10K/month have over 2000 designs listed and have been in the game several years. The average seller makes hundreds not thousands of dollars per month on this platform.

**In order to be successful in this endeavor, you must:**

- Choose a profitable Niche or Event.
- Create or Commission a unique design.
- Get the design approved by Amazon (there are content rules and copyright issues to learn).
- Create a compelling listing for the item.
- Sell a certain number of items in order to be allowed to list more items.
- Continue to upload designs regularly.
- Advertise to those items through social media or paid ads.

## Traffic Generation:

Awareness, Evaluation and Conversion: Amazon provides customers interested in buying products with unique designs. Your job lies in the awareness and evaluation stages. Are you the funniest "funny T-shirt for gardeners?" Did your listing have keywords customers might search for that other did not? This is not a traditional "apparel" purchase where someone is evaluating the quality of the shirt. The design is what sells the item. Yours must stand out to get the conversion. Note, frequently it has nothing to do with "art," it's about the message, often the simplest designs have the most success. Conversion is not an issue as Amazon is a trusted marketplace.

# MERCH BY AMAZON
## <u>MBA</u>

Degree of Difficulty to Learn

Upfront Costs ($)

Time to First Sale **1-2M**

Income Potential

How Hard to Drive Traffic

Medium

Builds Your Email List

Low

Risk Level

Low

# YOUR OWN E-COMMERCE STORE

If you don't want to sell on Amazon, you can create your own E-commerce Store. The advantage to this is that you own your own customers. You have their email list and can market to them again and again and again. The disadvantage is that you must drive traffic to your store. You are not Amazon, no one is typing your store name into their search bar and purchasing from you out of the blue. There are several types of stores you can create on your own:

- ♦ Churn and Burn Dropshipping
- ♦ Branded Dropshipping
- ♦ Private Label Dropshipping
- ♦ High Ticket Dropshipping
- ♦ Print on Demand
- ♦ Subscription Box Dropshipping

**Dropshipping** is a term that simply means, you do not pay the manufacturer for the item you are selling until the customer pays you for that item. You create a listing for the item on your store – Pictures and a Description- with a Buy Now button, then you send traffic (customers) to that product page, usually through paid ads on social media. A Shopper sees your ad, clicks the link, and buys your item. Automation allows for you to have a credit card on file with the manufacturer. The manufacturer sees the order, charges your card for the item, and ships the item off to your customer.

You have ZERO upfront inventory costs as you do not pay for the item until the customers pays you. You make your money by charging the customer more than it costs you to get the item from the manufacture and to advertise it to the consumer. (Quick basic easy math example: Item costs $5 from the manufacturer. You pay $10 in advertising costs to acquire a customer and you charge the customer $20 for the item. You have paid out $15 and brought in $20, clearing $5.) There are other costs involved such as the subscription fee for the platform and necessary Apps for the store, but essentially, the profit margins are between 20-30%.

You can use several platforms for this, Shopify and WooCommerce are two of the most popular ones. They provide you with a template that allows you to list your item for sale, accept credit cards for payment and attach "Apps" to your store that will take care of a myriad of necessities such as currency conversion if you want to sell worldwide, fulfillment so your vendors are automatically alerted there was a sale and begin the process of shipping the item to the customer and much more. Creating a listing is as easy as cutting and pasting and writing inside a text box.

The name of the game on this platform is getting eyes on your listings. Generating traffic through social media used to be very easy. Be wary of anyone offering to teach you dropshipping who does not show you CURRENT sales data and ALL of their back-end costs. Revenue is easy to generate, profit is another matter entirely. Get the whole story on any platform you are considering investing in, don't just rely on someone's purported sales proof.

# CHURN AND BURN DROPSHIPPING

Churn and Burn refers to a store that tests several products a week, trying to capitalize on trends or using software to see what other stores are selling successfully. They succeed through "Interruption Marketing." Sellers place ads on social media showing their item and hoping that the item is so compelling that it interrupts someone who looking at cat memes or posting their vacation pictures. The ad must stand out enough make them want to run and get their credit card. Essentially, they are the kiosk in the mall. Think of the real-world customer who drives to the local mall to go the Apple store and as she is walking through the mall, she sees a kiosk selling unicorn socks, that's not why she came to the mall, but suddenly she sees those socks and decides she can't live without them.

These stores were in their heyday in 2010-2020. The only thing needed was a traffic source and at that time, paid ads on social media were cheap and HIGHLY targeted. Ah, the good old days. Facebook reigned as the most sought-after traffic because they had been collecting so many data points about their users for years. It was creepy, yes, but a huge asset to advertisers. In 2021 when Apple iOS 15 allowed users to opt out of allowing their user data to be collected, the bottom fell out of Facebook advertising. Thousands of small businesses failed as a result of this update. Facebook did not have the data to allow extremely targeted ads to show to exactly who might buy their products anymore. Traffic simply became too expensive for these sellers.

These stores were generally selling items priced around $15-$40. With the cost of ads skyrocketing, it has become extremely difficult to test loads of low-cost items hoping to catch a trend and go viral. Dropshipping with the churn and burn model is not completely dead but it is not an easy path for new sellers and certainly not the gold rush it was in the mid-late 2000's.

Other social media platforms are being explored to try to re-create the heyday of pre-iOS Facebook and while many have success making sales on these platforms with these "trending products," very few have successfully scaled their business the way they did on Pre-iOS update Facebook. Sales will come in but generating consistent profit has eluded most dropshippers who are still following the 2017 model.

**In order to be successful in this endeavor, you must:**

- Find new and trending items to test on a regular basis.
- Create compelling listings (photos, ad copy) for those items on your stores.
- Constantly follow trends using software to see what others are selling.
- Optimize your site and product pages for good customer experience.
- Drive traffic to your store to attract buyers through social media or other sources.
- Deal with customer service and customer returns.
- Keep an email list of customers and constantly keep in touch with them.

## Traffic Generation:

Awareness, Evaluation and Conversion: You must create awareness for your offer, you must tell them about it in a way that is compelling, so they want to buy. Then you must have a website for them to buy from you that appears trustworthy so they do not feel like they will be scammed or cheated. You are responsible for all 3 stages of the customer's journey.

# DROPSHIPPING
## CHURN &BURN

Degree of Difficulty to Learn

Upfront Costs

$

Time to First Sale

**1M**

Income Potential

How Hard to Drive Traffic

High

Builds Your Email List

High

Risk Level

Low

# BRANDED DROPSHIPPING

One of the ways sellers who did not lose their businesses in that iOS update survived was to shift into what I call branded dropshipping. Creating a brand allows you to get traffic to your store over and over again from people who have already purchased from you. And since you are still dropshipping, you are still not buying inventory upfront. Many of the most successful stores online still dropship, they just have niched down and created a brand story, so customers seek them out after one purchase, i.e. without more paid ads. Kylie Jenner's beauty store is one example. Non-celebrity examples would include stores that have "niched down" to a passionate audience.

Let's say you create a store aimed at Cat Lovers. Customers buy something from the store after seeing an ad, which may actually cost you to lose some money upfront, as you just want them to become aware of your store. But after that sale, they keep returning because all of the items you sell are in the niche that they love. Further, they are getting emails for sales and promotions from you regularly that make them want to come back. The average lifetime value of the customer increases greatly. So, sellers can spend more on the initial ads as they are counting on repeat business. Sellers are still finding the items cheaply from a manufacturer and drop shipping them, they just stay in one niche and build a brand story instead of hopping on the latest trend. Because these sellers are selling items all in the same niche, upsells offered at checkout can also increase the average order value which defrays the rising advertising costs.

This model does take more time initially than chasing trends, as you will want a very nice website to display your goods. (In the churn and burn model a nice website is not as important as the ads go straight to the product page itself and frequently, customers do not even know the name of the store they are buying from). Your brand store needs a "look" and a "story" just like the brands real world shoppers know like Apple or Gucci. People will come to your store to shop, as opposed to only buying from you when they randomly see an ad for an item they like. This type of store allows you to build a loyal customer base, a highly targeted email list and an asset that you can sell once you have achieved a certain level of success.

You will need to find high quality suppliers who you will buy from again and again and who will keep you up to date on the newest items that are available in your niche. You will need to engage with customers and create promotions sales, and special events that make them want to return again and again. And initially you will have to invest in ads and influencers to draw attention to your store.

**In order to be successful in this endeavor, you must:**

- Creating a brand and brand story.
- Find items within your niche that will be high quality and still profitable.
- Optimize your site and product pages for good customer experience.
- Create compelling listings for those items on your stores.
- Drive traffic to your store to attract initial and new buyers
- Deal with customer service and customer returns.
- Keep an email list of customers and constantly keep in touch with them.

## Traffic Generation:

Awareness, Evaluation and Conversion: You must create awareness for your offer, you must tell them about it in a way that is compelling, so they want to buy. Then you must have a website for them to buy from you that appears trustworthy so they do not feel like they will be scammed or cheated. You are responsible for all 3 stages of the customer's journey.

# DROPSHIPPING
## <u>BRANDED STORE</u>

Degree of Difficulty to Learn

Upfront Costs

$(\$)(\$)$

Time to First Sale

**3M-4M**

Income Potential

Builds Your Email List

How Hard to Drive Traffic

High

Builds Your Email List

High

Risk Level

Low

# HIGH TICKET DROPSHIPPING

Believe it or not, you can sell very expensive items like hot tubs or "she sheds" from an online dropshipping store. These are not impulse items that you can advertise on social media sites like Facebook and Tik Tok. Because of their price point, consumers generally want to research these items before making a purchase. For this reason, these stores tend to advertise on Google and other specific websites that accept ads within their niche. Just like other dropshipping stores though, you do not have to pay for the item until the customer pays you. The issues for these types of store owners involve creating good relationships with suppliers and having a plan in place for returns as these can get complicated and eat away at your profits.

Similar to Branded Dropshipping stores, one must create a trustworthy and high-quality website. People are spending thousands of dollars on your item. The site must seem like all the big brand sites. Building a relationship with the right supplier can take time and effort but it is necessary for success. Ad costs may be higher than stores carrying lower cost items, but your Average Order Value is high enough that you can spend much more to acquire customers.

This type of store can also serve as a branded dropshipping store. Once you have success in selling a high-ticket item in a particular niche, you can offer low-cost accessories to those same customers you have already paid to acquire. For example, let's say you choose to focus on high end Barbeques that sell for $2,000 or more. Once a customer purchases that item, you can offer them BBQ lights, mats, gloves, or utensils. These low-ticket offerings are icing on the cake and can generate easy extra income as you have already paid to acquire that customer so profit margins on these items are much higher.

**In order to be successful in this endeavor, you must:**

- Choose the right product (one in high demand that can be sourced cheaply enough to turn a profit).
- Develop a good relationship with a supplier of that product.
- Have a plan in place for returns and refunds.
- Build a professional looking website
- Create a compelling listing for the product.
- Create a compelling Ad.
- Get that ad show up in Google shopping or on another site where purchasers would research.
- Deal with customer service.
- Keep an email list of customers and constantly keep in touch with them.
- Create offers for "accessories" within the niche to offer to current customers.

## Traffic Generation:

Awareness, Evaluation and Conversion: You must create awareness for your offer, you must tell them about it in a way that is compelling, so they want to buy. Then you must have a website for them to buy from you that appears trustworthy so they do not feel like they will be scammed or cheated. You are responsible for all 3 stages of the customer's journey.

# DROPSHIPPING
## HIGH TICKET STORE

Degree of Difficulty to Learn

BEG-INT

Upfront Costs

$ $

Time to First Sale

**2M-3M**

Income Potential

Income Potential

How Hard to Drive Traffic

**High**

Builds Your Email List

**High**

Risk Level

**Low**

# PRINT ON DEMAND STORES

Much like Amazon Merch there are other print on demand (POD) platforms that will host your designs and allow you to sell from their website. They do not have Amazon traffic. The profit margins tend to be higher, and you own your own customers. Some examples of these platforms include Gearbubble and Etsy for all sorts of items and Shine On for jewelry and watches. Some of these platforms give you the option of selling directly from a storefront that lives on their website or creating your own

## E-commerce store on a site like Shopify.

With the latter option, those platforms have Apps that allow for very simple product uploads and automated fulfillment. Personally, I will always opt for my own store as I want to 100% own my assets and my customer list. If I have a Shopify print on demand store and have a best-selling "Cat" T-shirt, it is very easy for me to source "Cat" related items, like toys and scratch posts and offer them on my own platform to those customers I have already paid to acquire with my initial T-shirt sale. The concept for these stores is very similar to the branded dropshipping stores explained above.

Sites like Etsy were originally created to sell handmade items and these items do very well there as shoppers come looking for unique one of a kind offers and are willing to pay more than they would from Amazon due to its originality. But one does not need to create handmade items to use the Etsy marketplace. Many sellers dropship from Etsy as well. This requires items that "seem unique" like jewelry and home goods that might appeal to someone already on the Etsy platform.

Gearbubble and Shine On allow a seller to sell items that are original to those platforms but that can also be customized by the seller or consumer to make them original. For example, an item like a heart necklace can be sold by anyone on the platform, but a creative seller can design a unique "message card" that can be placed inside the necklace's gift box. That card can be a special birthday greeting you created or can be customized by the consumer with the recipient's name for instance.

While these platforms make it super simple to sell their wares and designs you create yourself, the difficulty lies in getting traffic to those listings. So, in essence, customization is sort of a cross between a churn and burn dropshipping store, capitalizing on trends and holidays and events while staying within a particular niche. For those with already successful branded stores however, the addition of these items with designs you create within your brand niche can be a gold mine of additional offerings.

**In order to be successful in this endeavor, you must:**

- Creating a design in a niche or series of niches.
- Upload them to your store or the platform's storefront with a compelling listing.
- Optimize your site and product pages for good customer experience.
- Drive traffic to your store to attract buyers.
- Deal with customer service and customer returns.
- Keep an email list of customers and constantly keep in touch with them.

## Traffic Generation:

Awareness, Evaluation and Conversion: You must create awareness for your offer, you must tell them about it in a way that is compelling, so they want to buy. Then you must have a website for them to buy from you that appears trustworthy so they do not feel like they will be scammed or cheated. You are responsible for all 3 stages of the customer's journey.

# DROPSHIPPING
# PRINT ON DEMAND STORE

Degree of Difficulty to Learn

BEG-INT

Upfront Costs

$

Time to First Sale

**1M-3M**

Income Potential

How Hard to Drive Traffic

High

Builds Your Email List

High

Risk Level

Low

# SUBSCRIPTION BOX STORES

A more recent trend in the e-commerce store space is stores that offer subscription boxes. These are very highly niched stores. The attraction of these stores is that sellers get Recurring Monthly Revenue (RMR).

RMR should be a goal for anyone selling online. First, consistent monthly income allows for growth and expansion as well as peace of mind. Second, you have a community of people to whom you could sell other items. And finally, if you are keen on exiting your business and selling your store in the future, RMR considerably increases the sale price you will command.

Examples of subscription boxes might be a once-a-month "Beauty Box" where you contract with a distributor to source and "kit" (assemble several items into one box) and ship different beauty items every month. You create a community within your chosen niche, through paid ads, blogging or social media groups and you create a demand for a monthly gift box. Passionate niches work best such as rescue dog lovers, crafters, or preppers for example. The engagement within the community keeps people interested in the subject and the anticipation of something new and surprising keeps them subscribed. This of course takes time to build and time to find the materials at a reasonable price, as well as a warehouse that will kit and mail the items, but the benefits can be lucrative and long term.

Similar to Branded Dropshipping stores this requires you to find and appeal to a passionate audience. Then you will have to source and have kitted boxes containing the items you will ship out monthly. You will need to engage with that audience via email, social media groups or influencers to keep them interested in and anticipating the next shipment so they will happily renew their membership.

**In order to be successful in this endeavor, you must:**

- Find a niche you and others are passionate about.
- Create a group or compelling content that offers value and encourages engagement.
- Create a website or Social Media group for the niche.
- Find items the group is passionate about at a cost that will ensure monthly profit.
- Find a reliable supplier to source, kit and store your items to be shipped directly to customers.
- Drive traffic to your group through ads or incentives or word of mouth.
- Deal with customer service and customer returns.
- Keep an email list of customers and constantly keep in touch with them.

## Traffic Generation:

Awareness, Evaluation and Conversion: You must create awareness for your offer, you must tell them about it in a way that is compelling, so they want to buy. Then you must have a website for them to buy from you that appears trustworthy so they do not feel like they will be scammed or cheated. You are responsible for all 3 stages of the customer's journey.

# DROPSHIPPING
## SUBSCRIPTION BOX STORES

Degree of Difficulty to Learn

BEG-INT

Upfront Costs ⑤⑤

Time to First Sale **3M-6M**

Income Potential 💰💰💰

How Hard to Drive Traffic

High

Builds Your Email List

High

Risk Level

Low

# PRIVATE LABEL STORES

Another type of E-commerce store is a branded private label store. This does not involve dropshipping as upfront inventory costs are required. This is a little different then just branding your store to be in one niche. It is a store that includes items that are unique to you in some way, either you invented the item, or you tweaked an existing item in some way as to make it unique. This is less frequent and often done in connection with private label selling on Amazon. The item may be the same, and you are allowed to sell it on both your store and Amazon at the same time, but you get to keep the customers data and market to them again and again. You do not need an Amazon listing for this though, but to fulfill without an Amazon listing, you would need a manufacturer or 3PL Warehouse who is willing to store your inventory and send them out, one a time, to your customers as they are purchased. The benefit of having a listing concurrently on Amazon is that you can fulfill through Amazon itself.

This takes the same amount of time and effort as becoming a 3rd party seller on Amazon and is really recommended for folks already selling on Amazon as it's a second traffic source and an opportunity to have your own customer list. For people thinking of doing this instead of selling on Amazon, expect to spend as much time and effort as a 3rd party Amazon seller would to get started and even more time and effort driving traffic to your site and finding a supplier willing to store and ship out items one at a time. This requires significant upfront costs for inventory to be bought in bulk as well.

**In order to be successful in this endeavor, you must:**

- Choose the right product (one in high demand that can be sourced cheaply enough to turn a profit).
- Build a branded store for that item and niche.
- Design the packaging or tweak the product so that it is unique to you in some way.
- Source the product from a manufacturer – pay upfront for inventory.
- Create a compelling listing for the product.
- Fulfill the item through your own Amazon listing or through your own Manufacturer.
- Drive traffic to your store with paid ads or other sources.
- Deal with customer service and customer returns.
- Keep an email list of customers and constantly keep in touch with them.

## Traffic Generation:

Awareness, Evaluation and Conversion: You must create awareness for your offer, you must tell them about it in a way that is compelling, so they want to buy. Then you must have a website for them to buy from you that appears trustworthy so they do not feel like they will be scammed or cheated. You are responsible for all 3 stages of the customer's journey.

# PRIVATE LABEL STORE

Degree of Difficulty to Learn INT-ADV

Upfront Costs $ $ $ $

Time to First Sale **8M-12M**

Income Potential

How Hard to Drive Traffic
High

Builds Your Email List
High

Risk Level
High

# E-COMMERCE WRAP UP

As you can see, there are a myriad of ways one can sell physical products online. Some provide the traffic but don't let you keep your own customer data; others allow you to fully own and control your own store. Keeping 100% of your customers data is a huge benefit, but then you are required to generate all the traffic to those stores on your own. I have often said, Amazon is a traffic source and not a business. There are workarounds you can use to get your customer's data from Amazon sales, such as warranty sign-ups and product inserts, some are compliant with Amazon's terms of service, and some are not. One can now sell their Amazon store so it is an asset, but at the end of the day, you are building your castle in Amazon's sandbox and must be ready and able to pivot as their policies and terms of service change.

Many dropshippers who relied solely on Facebook ads were devastated when Apple nixed default data collection on mobile devices. Facebook too is a traffic source, not a business. And as large and successful Facebook is as a company, they too built a portion of their business in someone else's sandbox, namely, Apple's. And they paid the price. Facebook lost millions of dollars because they had relied so heavily on Apple for mobile users' personal data. When that was taken away, Facebook had to change their entire algorithm for matching advertisers with their desired customers.

All of these platforms have pros and cons. Sellers must go into them with their eyes open and be ready to pivot to Plan B when updates and new policies dramatically change the playing field. If all this seems daunting, read on. There are a great many other ways to create an online income stream and, in the chapters, to follow we will explore those in detail.

# CHAPTER 2

---

# AFFILIATE MARKETING

Affiliate marketing refers to selling someone else's products or services. You're not creating the product yourself, sourcing the product yourself or offering the services yourself. You are the middleman, selling something that someone else has created in exchange for a referral fee. There are several sites that aggregate vendors who are actively looking for affiliates to promote their offers. Two well-known ones, for example, include ClickBank and MaxWeb. The former offers everything from $10 eBooks to medical supplements that cost hundreds of dollars. The vendors are willing to give an affiliate a percentage of the sale they generate, anywhere from 10% to 100%.

Why would a vendor give an affiliate all the money he earned from the sale? Because the vendor knows the lifetime value of that customer is worth far more than that first sale and is willing to invest in a "loss" upfront to reap future profits. Two types of Affiliate Income are referred to as Revenue Share (Rev Share) and Cost per Action (CPA).

Cost per Action is a one-time payment a vendor gives you for sending them a lead or a sale. If you drive traffic to an insurance firm, you might get paid per incoming call or per customer. A small fee is paid to you if you send them a qualified lead and a larger fee is paid to you if they "close the sale" to that lead. Revenue Share is just as it sounds. For instance, if you drive traffic to a vitamin supplement company, you can get paid, not only a percentage of that first sale, but also a percentage of the recurring orders when a customer chooses to refill their vitamins.

In a CPA offers for supplements, some companies who only charge $30 a bottle may be willing to give you $100 for the first sale, even though they might lose money, because they are not giving you a percentage of their recurring revenue and they believe that will generate more profit to them in the long run. Many vendors will give you the option to take CPA or Revenue share. The benefit of CPA offers is that returned items are not deducted from your payouts. The benefit of Revenue Share is the potential to generate more revenue beyond the first sale with recurring payouts when a buyer re-orders.

People who create digital products, like a video series on "How to Train Your Misbehaving Dog" are happy to pay you to help them sell those videos. The creator only had to put in the work one time to make the videos. A sale is as simple to fulfill as sending the customer an email with a link to download their purchase and even that is automated. So, if the sale price is $300 for the series, when a vendor pays you $150 for that sale, they aren't "losing" $150 of that sale, they are "gaining" $150 from a sale they otherwise would not have made without you. If that same vendor offers a monthly subscription to a group or newsletter, they may also offer you a percentage of their "backend," so you can benefit from the recurring income as well.

Affiliate marketing is one of the easiest ways to create an online income stream. But despite what the carnival barkers out there scream from their Tik Tok and YouTube Videos, it is NOT "passive income." If you set up a site online that makes an offer to a popular item, be it a $3000 video course showing folks how to make millions in crypto currency or a supplement promising to cure disease, and you do nothing else, that offer will live in utter obscurity on the world wide web as no one will see it, ever, no one, ever. You must **work to generate traffic** to your site so that you can refer those people to profitable offers.

The good news is in most instances of affiliate marketing, you are not responsible for closing the sale, but rather for generating awareness and interest in the offer. Awareness traffic is easier to generate than conversion traffic because you are simply asking for them to *click over to someone's offer*, not to take out a credit card and purchase on the spot. It is up to the vendor to close the sale.

You must continuously generate traffic to your offers online in this business. This is infinitely doable, but it still involves work on your part. Whether that involves content creation (blog posts, ad copy, videos) or paid advertising, you must create the content and create ads that you want to use to run traffic to your offer page. Remember, the entire ecosphere of online income relies on generating traffic to offers and building an email list. Those are the fundamental core concepts of any online business.

Generating traffic is the most easily accomplished using paid ads, but there are other what we call "organic" ways to generate traffic to an offer. You can use all of these methods to sell a variety of affiliate offers. The beauty of affiliate marketing is that once the sale closes and you get sent your commission, your work is done. You have no customer services issues at all. You don't deal with complaints, returns or any post-sale issues. In this way it is more "passive" than selling and supporting your own offers. One can create a successful affiliate marketing business working part time but as with most endeavors, the more work (content creation) you put in, the more profits you will attain.

## Here are the four main sources for traffic to affiliate offers:

**Paid Ads:** Buy ads on social media or major websites touting the offer.

**Website/Newsletter/Podcasts:** Create Content on some platform that attracts people in a particular niche and send them to offers for vendor's products.

**Email Marketing:** Create content around a specific niche and offer a Lead Magnet for an Email Address, then email that list over and over again with valuable content that includes offers.

**Influencer:** Creating content around a niche and get brands and vendors to pay you for an endorsement.

# AFFILIATE MARKETING PAID ADS

Once you decide on an offer you want to promote, the high-ticket vendors will generally provide you with marketing materials to help you promote their offer through organic content creation or paid ads. Some material will be fancy pictures, banners, or videos. Others will just show you their sales letters and ask that you create your own ads based on their information. When you are using paid ads for high ticket offers (one that will generate commissions over $1000) keep in mind that vendors who offer these affiliate deals are generally very, very good marketers with extensively tested ad copy on their product pages aimed at closing deals. Your job in that situation is not to make the sale; it is to generate enough interest in the offer that the prospect clicks through from your website to the vendors offer page. Let the information on that page close the sale. For lower ticket offers, like less expensive digital training or physical products, you content will both introduce and close the deal.

Ads can be placed on any social media site (though some restrict ads for certain offers like gambling, crypto, tobacco and other topics). Ads can be text or video based. They may be banners you pay to have appear on sites like CNN or Fox News that may catch a reader's attention as they scroll through stories. Or they may be long form stories you place on Facebook ads detailing some journey from point A to point B (fat to skinny, broke to rich) that you write to relate to your target audience and pique their curiosity.

Video ads have been very successful in the affiliate space. On average they run 30 seconds to 3 minutes long depending on the platform they will appear on. One can create video ads to promote on YouTube, Tik Tok, FB Reels and more.

Do not shy away from this opportunity because you fear video. *You never have to be the one on camera and you personally do not have to endorse any items.*

For instance, if you wanted to promote a weight loss supplement, you could start a YouTube channel called "Healthy You," create a corresponding website with a page that holds the offer. Create a video ad that has pictures and narration aimed at enticing the viewer to click through to your site, see the offer and click through to the Vendor's sale page. If that seems daunting, understand that the first time you create a YouTube channel, it may take you 30 minutes, the next time, it will take you 10. The first time you create a website page, it may take you a whole hour. The next time if may take you 15 minutes. If you can't fathom creating those, both can be done for you online for about $50-$150 all in.

Your name is not on the site. Your face is not on camera. You are not the one making or endorsement the offer, you are the one explaining the offer. Of course, if you want to have your face on camera and you want to endorse and offer, that is great and also can be quite effective for certain offers, especially if you have a certain expertise, but it is not necessary at all.

Copywriting, writing the text for your advertising, is key in paid ads. Whether in video scripts or text ads, how you say what you say is crucial. This is a skill you can learn, and once you are immersed in affiliate marketing you will see thousands of examples of successful ad copy that you can model.

Commissions on affiliate items vary dramatically depending on what you are promoting. A sale of a short guide, sent to the consumer in digital format can generate a commission as low as $10. A sale of a $3000 course could generate commission of $1200 - $1500 and a sale of a $10,000 coaching offer could be as high as $2500 to $4,000. Many programs have several offerings, such a starter plan for members at $30/month and then mid-ticket $2500 courses and finally high-ticket that can generate $3000-$4000.

You see, those sellers offering the $30/month programs are working hard to "upsell" those buyers into higher and higher cost programs that they also offer. The beauty of promoting these types of programs is that the first sale is fairly easy to close because it's such a small investment. And that buyer "is tagged as yours" throughout their whole journey with that seller, so you would get commissions on every upsell as well. These are the types of offers that can generate a lot of money, even for brand new affiliates.

**In order to be successful in this endeavor, you must:**

- Find a high-quality offer to sell from a reputable vendor.

- Write compelling ad copy that speaks specifically to your target customer.

- Create content that showcases that offer (video or text).

- Create a Landing Page (website or funnel page) that will house that content.

- Decide on a platform to advertise on that is congruent with where your prospects gather.

- Drive traffic to that ad through paid platforms.

- Continue to update and refresh your content to successful offers.

## Traffic Generation:

Awareness, Evaluation and Conversion: You are responsible for step one, awareness. Your content and/or your ads are aimed at people in the particular niche you chose. The goal is to get those folks to become aware of the specific offer you are promoting in that niche and get them to click through to the vendors site so the vendor can close the sale. The vendor is responsible for closing the deal with their sales page or product listing and they are responsible for the conversion.

# AFFILIATE MARKETING
## <u>PAID ADS</u>

Degree of Difficulty to Learn | BEG-INT

Upfront Costs | $ $

Time to First Sale | **1M-3M**

Income Potential | $ $ $ $

How Hard to Drive Traffic | Medium

Builds Your Email List | High

Risk Level | Low

# AFFILIATE MARKETING WEBSITE/NEWSLETTER/PODCASTER

This category essential covers content creation that is aimed at a particular niche.

I have called it website/newsletter/podcaster, but I am referring to anything that allows you to have a platform that provides ongoing access to people in your chosen niche. The niche can be very narrow like "Labradoodle owners" or really broad like "making money online."

Let's say you chose Labradoodles. You could create a website in which you post articles reviewing products for these dogs. Within those articles you would discuss various products or services that might appeal to labradoodle owners. These articles would include an "affiliate link" a hyper link that is embedded with a code that tells the vendor the sale came from your review site, not someone else's site (this link created by the vendor, and you need only cut and paste it into your site).

Review sites are the most common form of this content as they purport to Review, Rank or Compare different items and then lead the reader to select one or more, each with your special link, to purchase. The vendors for these offers are everywhere, even Amazon will let you send traffic to their site and give you a commission for each sale. This method relies on creating content on a regular basis that offers value to your audience and finding products to promote that are congruent to your niche.

As an example, let's say you are reviewing glow in the dark collars for dogs. You recommend a certain type and link to that item that is for sale on Amazon. If the reader buys that collar, you would get not only a commission on the sale of the collar alone, but also on the other items the shopper purchased on that visit and all visits within the next 24 hours. While affiliate commission on Amazon range from .5 to 10% of the purchase depending on the type of item purchased. The average affiliate on Amazon earns between .5 and 1% of the sale.

There are many vendors beside Amazon that will pay you a percentage per sale and if you find a good high-ticket digital product that might appeal to your audience you can make $1000-$2000 or more for a single referral. A good place to start to find offers for your niche is to search in the site ClickBank which aggregates vendors who are looking for affiliates. Just type a keyword about your niche into the search bar and you will be shown hundreds of items to promote.

A newsletter is the same idea but offered through email instead. Podcasting takes a bit more time to learn but this platform allows you to speak to people in your niche, have special guests and even take advertising from vendors who want to reach your audience. Many Social Media sites allow for the creation of private groups that people who share a similar interest can join. Through posting regularly in these groups, keeping up engagement with your audience and providing value you can post specific offers in the group that will generate sales for your vendors.

Note that while this field is a great way to drive traffic to your affiliate offers, you must still get *initial traffic* to your website or newsletter or podcast. Generating frequent and engaging content will be noticed by content curation platforms such as Tik Tok and sites like Google or YouTube will display popular content more frequently and higher up in their search engines. Paid Ads will always be quicker for getting offers noticed but if you have a very niche specific, patience and have well-researched keywords to include in your material that are relevant for your buyers, your content could get noticed "organically."

You can also hire companies to help you "rank" your sites, so they are shown first when people are searching in your niche topic.

**In order to be successful in this endeavor, you must:**

- Spend time creating content for your site, or newsletter, podcast, or group.
- Regularly engage with your audience and provide value to keep them interested.
- Find high quality reliable offers from trusted vendors to promote.
- Research relevant keywords to use in your content to try to "rank" your site on search engines.
- Create compelling content around those offers that entice people to click through to the offer.
- Continue creating unique content that ensures people stay in your group.
- Continue to find new and unique offers to promote.

## Traffic Generation:

Awareness, Evaluation and Conversion: You are responsible for step one, awareness. Your content and/or your ads are aimed at people in the particular niche you chose. The goal is to get those folks to become aware of the specific offer you are promoting in that niche and get them to click through to the vendors site so the vendor can close the sale. The vendor is responsible for evaluation and conversion.

# AFFILIATE MARKETING
## WEBSITE/NEWSLETTER/PODCASTER

Degree of Difficulty to Learn | BEG-INT

Upfront Costs | ($)

Time to First Sale | **2M-3M**

Income Potential

How Hard to Drive Traffic | Medium

Builds Your Email List | High

Risk Level | Low

# AFFILIATE MARKETING
# EMAIL MARKETING

When I first started researching making money online back in 2013, there was a mantra I saw everywhere: "The money is in the list." When you build an email list of people interested in a particular niche, you can market offers to them over and over again. The rule of thumb is said to be that each person on your email list, if marketed to effectively is worth $1/month. That may sound small but if you have a super-engaged email list of 5,000 people, that can be a full-time income on its own for many people.

Email marketing is not free, but it is highly affordable. You must acquire an email list and then get a marketing automation service with autoresponders. These services store your email list and schedule and automate sending emails to your list in bulk. The companies that provide these services charge by the number of people on your list and how often you email them. So, while the prices can get quite high for thousands of emails, by the time you have thousands of emails, you are generating thousands of dollars and the cost is easily justified. At first, plans start at around $20/month.

Once you have an email list, you can send them offers all the time. It is not unheard of for marketers to send prospects on their email list a DAILY email. That is not necessary but the more you mail, the more you make, so long as you are providing valuable content in those emails, and not just spammy emails with nothing but offers.

But how can you create a business based on emails if you don't have a list? This is where the "ethical bribe" comes in.

It is also called a Lead Magnet. You create something of value for your prospects, something at that attracts them. For instance, let's say you are focused on the gardening niche. You might create an

eBook about best practices for the home gardener. You could offer that product for a small price or even free in order to get interested customers to give you their email address so you could send them that eBook. This way you would acquire a list of people who you now know are interested in gardening. You would then email them with tips and resources and recommend products to them in that niche within these emails. Of course, the content must be original and valuable to them.

It does not take a whole eBook in most cases. Marketing to Dog Lovers, you could create a list of "20 Foods You Should Never Feed Your Dogs," spruced up with good graphics so it would look very professional. In that case, the perceived value doesn't have to be $20, just high enough for someone to say, I want to know that information so much that I will put my email in the box that says Download the List Now.

Once you have that email, you can scour ClickBank for offers relevant to dog owners, or review Amazon items for dog lover and tell them which is the best of those offers with a link to buy. Spend time on the Lead Magnet creation, it is your first contact with your audience, your calling card as it were, and it should truly provide value and insight.

Once you create the Lead Magnet however, you are not done. You can write the best eBook, record the greatest Video training or write the best most helpful cheat sheet, but if you do not drive traffic to that content, the cheat sheet, eBook or video series will live on the world wide web in utter obscurity.

Paid ads are the quickest and easiest way to bring traffic to your offer. But there are other ways to get eyes on it as well, such as hiring an influencer in the field to tout your offer or contacting groups online you think would want a free copy of what you have as a gift to their audience.

Guest posting on other people's blog with posts that offer valuable information to their audience can help establish your authority and get you new followers. You can also create content on YouTube or TikTok or similar sites that offers valuable content and attracts followers. Once you have the followers you can offer them a newsletter or the lead magnet that will turn them from social media follower to an email marketing prospect.

**In order to be successful in this endeavor, you must:**

- Spend time creating your Lead Magnet.
- Decide how to generate traffic to the Lead Magnet.
- Write ad copy or proposals to podcast hosts/website owners/influencers for your Lead Magnet.
- Sign up for and Set Up your autoresponder.
- Drive traffic to your Lead Magnet.
- Fulfill the orders for your Lead Magnet.
- Find valuable and high-quality leads from vetted vendors to promote.
- Write compelling emails that will encourage readers to click through to the vendor's sale page.
- Continue to engage with your list and offer value not just offers.

## Traffic Generation:

Awareness, Evaluation and Conversion: You are responsible for step one, awareness. The content of your emails is aimed at people in the particular niche you chose. The goal is to get those folks to become aware of the specific offer you are promoting in that niche and get them to click through to the vendors site so the vendor can close the sale. The vendor is responsible for steps evaluation and conversion.

# AFFILIATE MARKETING
## EMAIL LIST

Degree of Difficulty to Learn

BEG

Upfront Costs

$

Time to First Sale

**3M-4M**

Income Potential

How Hard to Drive Traffic

**Medium**

Builds Your Email List

**High**

Risk Level

**Low**

# AFFILIATE MARKETING INFLUENCER

Contrary to popular belief, you don't have to be 23 years old with a bikini body to be an influencer online. The ones that you may be thinking of when you see the word "influencer" are extreme examples. But everyday folks from all walks of life are influencers. This type of affiliate marketing is the least expensive but the most labor intensive. Essentially, you start a channel on You Tube, or an Instagram account or post hundreds of short videos on Tik Tok or Reels, all within the same topic. You create content that teaches someone about your niche, i.e. How to apply eyeliner correctly, or answers folks' questions, like "What is the best time of year to plant tomatoes?" Or coach them in the "5 most common mistake new pickleball players make and how to avoid them."

Once you get a decent following, small brands may reach out to you for "shout outs" (mentioning their product in your next few posts) or reviews or endorsements. There are sites that aggregate influencers and match them with vendors who are looking for folks in their niche to promote their products. Of course, you don't have to wait for vendors to reach out to you.

You can use the same system explained above to find an offer on ClickBank, then suggest it to your followers and collect an affiliate commission. You can also reach out to vendors, other content creators like podcasters and bloggers and work out some revenue share offer. Note, this differs from making offer specific content on social media sites or in your various websites where you have avatars and anonymous content. You are focused exclusively on one niche and you are personally the one promoting it as yourself, your face, your reputation, you.

This strategy is a longer-term play, requiring loads of content. It is extremely low cost financially and has little risk other than wasted time and potentially bruised ego if you fail miserably. This should be probably be undertaken only if you really have a passion for what you are creating content about, as you will need to stay motivated and energetic in your content and its creation.

Even though most media is focused on young people being influencers, there are several examples of very successful older influencers that don't get the press, teaching a skill that brings them in a very nice income. For instance, DIY experts, financial experts, nutritionists, travel experts.

Type "[your expertise] + the word "influencer" into YouTube and you will see many everyday folks creating videos that offer value and have a decent sized following that they successfully monetize.

The more content on the more channels you create, the greater your perceived authority in the field, the greater your following will become, and the more money you can demand to promote products and services.

**In order to be successful in this endeavor, you must:**

- Create an account on your platform of choice.
- Create tons of content establishing yourself as a trustworthy exert or source of knowledge.
- Reach out to businesses offering your services or find compelling ClickBank offers.
- Sign up for Sites that matchmake vendors and influencers.
- Continue to create tons of content and keep followers engaged so they keep coming back.

## Traffic Generation:

Awareness, Evaluation and Conversion: You are responsible for step one, awareness. Your content and your endorsements are aimed at people in the particular niche you chose. The goal is to get those folks to become aware of the specific offer you are promoting in that niche and get them to click through to the vendors site so the vendor can close the sale. The vendors are responsible for evaluation and conversion.

# AFFILIATE MARKETING
## <u>INFLUENCER</u>

Degree of Difficulty to Learn

Upfront Costs $

Time to First Sale **4M-8M**

Income Potential

How Hard to Drive Traffic

**Medium-High**

Builds Your Email List

**Medium**

Risk Level

**Low**

# CHAPTER 3

---

# GIG WORK

The easiest way to make your first dollar online is to offer your time for money. Advertise a skill you have either by listing on a gig work site, placing ads online, or by word of mouth in relevant groups. You can ask for an hourly rate or a flat fee rate to deliver that service. If you want to see the wide variety of services people offer online then check out the site Fiverr.com (yes, 2 R's).

The things that people are getting paid for on this site are mind blowing and not all are related to "business." There are fun services like the fellow who will wish your friend Happy Birthday in the voice of Morgan Freeman. And there are truly bizarre ones like the fellow who will record himself shouting your name into a bush for $5. (By the by, that guy had several Five Star reviews. If you consider that only a small portion of users who actually leave a review, then clearly, he had at least some takers!) Now, these types of gigs are not going to allow you to retire by any means, but they are a good insight into side hustles people have created.

For our purposes, the real money to be made in gig work is similar to "temp work" in the real world and services aimed at online business owners are the most popular. Here is a non-exhaustive list of some services I have used since starting my Online journey:

- Website Builder
- Funnel Builder
- Transcriber
- Book Cover Designer
- E-book Formatter
- Copy Writer
- Social Media Manager
- Search Engine Optimization
- Content Creator
- Customer Service Assistant

There are hundreds more services that online business owners need and will pay you to do. In order to get this type of work, the easiest path is to sign up for a site like Fiverr (see also Upwork and "HireMyMom" as other examples). You may already have a skill that is in demand, but you can also learn a skill that is in demand.

Nearly anyone can learn a few of the services I have outsourced, such as transcription and book cover design. In fact, with Artificial Intelligence (AI) software, transcription has become so much easier than in the past. You simply take the recorded file and upload it to a site like Otter.ai. The site will create a text file of the recording. You then have to edit the finished product for spelling and grammar accuracy. AI is not perfect yet, so there will be some funky mistakes but if will save hours of time allowing you to simply edit a file rather than start from scratch with a blank page.

For book cover design, see a site called Canva, which has templates and easy to use drag and drop features that allow folks with zero artistic talent to produce some great graphics and book covers that they can offer for sale. Canva has excellent free tutorial videos on their site as well and a site called Udemy has advanced classes for under $50 that can teach even the least gifted artists how to use the templates.

Gig Work is an easy way to learn how to make your first money online and gain confidence in the fact that people will pay for your services. I know many people coming into the make money online space just don't really believe that online income is possible, gig work is a simple way to prove the concept. For some people, the idea of starting a business is daunting, but they still want some of the freedom that comes from working from home. Full time Gig Work is possible. You are still trading your time for dollars, so it is not possible to "scale" your income beyond the numbers of hours in a day you are willing to work. But you lose the commute, make your own hours and have more freedom in determining how you spend your days.

The work is obviously not as stable as a 9-5 but if you can create a real demand for your services you can stay booked throughout the month. I would not recommend this as an option for those truly interested in creating an online business but if you are currently unemployed or under employed, this is certainly an avenue to look into.

**In order to be successful in this endeavor, you must:**

- ◆ Create an account on a platform like Fiverr.com.

- ◆ Optimize your service offering listing by explaining why you are the one to hire.

- ◆ Coordinate your schedule to deliver the services you promised accurately and on time.

- ◆ Advertise your services online in posts on social media and ask friends for referrals.

- ◆ Consistently deliver timely and excellent work product to earn reviews and repeat customers.

## Traffic Generation:

Awareness, Evaluation and Conversion: The aggregator sites out there have categories for different skills. Consumers are already aware that they need a service, your job lies in the Evaluation stage. You must stand out among other service providers so that they choose you. This is done by creating a compelling listing and getting early reviews. Conversions are taken care of by the site whose reputation and safeguards assure against worries of being scammed or cheated.

# GIG WORKER

Degree of Difficulty to Learn **BEG**

Upfront Costs **0-$**

Time to First Sale **1M-2M**

Income Potential

How Hard to Drive Traffic **Medium**

Builds Your Email List **Low**

Risk Level **Low**

# CHAPTER 4

---

# AGENCY/DROPSERVICING

If you want to turn Gig Work into your own business, then there is the option of opening an Agency and hiring these workers yourself. Most folks new to online marketing think of being an Agency Owner as overwhelming. This is why I refer to this plan as "Dropservicing." Just as in E-commerce, when we purchased an item from a manufacturer or wholesale distributor and then resold that item to a customer online, in this instance we simply purchase the gigs from freelancers and resell their work product to a business owner.

Let me give you a very basic example. Let's say you decide to create a team of transcribers and make a listing on one of these sites advertising transcription services. You would put together a team of vetted transcribers online (this would require prep work of vetting them for accuracy and efficiency). You would find ones that would transcribe a 10-minute audio clip for $5- $10 as an example. Your listing would offer a 10-minute audio clip for $15-20. The business owner would hire you, pay you the $15-20 and you would turn around and hire a gig worker for $5-$10. Eventually you could build a team of these workers and even progress to hiring a project manager to coordinate all the workers and you could just focus on supervising the manager and growing the agency.

Obviously, this is a very simplified example, but it is a way to become an online business owner without taking expensive courses and investing a lot of money upfront. Nearly any work offered online can be resold in this fashion. The key is do this with offers you understand, even if you are not an expert. Workers must be vetted, and you will need several workers lined up as you grow because many of these workers could find other jobs or leave the platform and they must be replaced.

**In order to be successful in this endeavor, you must:**

- Choose a type of gig work you want to specialize in.
- Create an account on a platform like Fiverr.com.
- Audition several online workers to find ones that consistently produce quality work.
- Optimize your service offering listing by explaining why you are the one to hire.
- Advertise your services online in posts on social media and ask friends for referrals.
- Continue to vet new workers.
- Insure that your workers are continually producing high quality timely results for your clients.

## Traffic Generation:

Awareness, Evaluation and Conversion: The aggregator sites out there have categories for different skills. Consumers are already aware that they need a service, your job lies in the Evaluation stage. You must stand out among other service providers so that they choose you. Conversions are taken care of by the site whose reputation and safeguards assure against worries of being scammed or cheated.

# DROPSERVICING / AGENCY

Degree of Difficulty to Learn

Upfront Costs

Time to First Sale **1M-2M**

Income Potential

How Hard to Drive Traffic

Medium

Builds Your Email List

Low

Risk Level

Low

# CHAPTER 5

# BOOKS

There are three main ways you can use books to make money online:

♦ **Self-Publishing** Write or commission to have written a book and publish it on the Amazon KDP Platform.

♦ **Low Content or No Content Books** Create and publish coloring books, puzzle books and journals on KDP.

♦ **Publish** other people's book on Amazon.

## SELF-PUBLISHING BOOKS

Amazon's platform for books is known as Kindle Direct Publishing or KDP. It is not the only platform for authors to self-publish, but it is the easiest and most well-known. It allows authors to upload a manuscript onto their platform so long as its properly formatted, and create e-books, paperback books and hardcover books that can be printed on demand, one at a time, and sent to customers. Authors no longer need to spend years convincing agents to represent them and publishing houses to publish their masterpiece. Once you have the formatted manuscript, you can put it up for sale on the Amazon Marketplace in under 10 minutes. Amazon takes up to 72 hours to approve your book and then it is live and ready for sales to come in.

Your book can be found by interested shoppers on Amazon by the keywords you choose to describe the book, or by ads that you place on the Amazon Marketplace yourself. You can also advertise to the book on social media just like any physical item you wanted to sell. Once the buyer purchases the book, Amazon prints it, sends it to the customer and you get your cut of the sale price. As you set the price of your book and you will see the amount Amazon will take and the amount you will keep as profit. Their cut depends on the length and type of the book you are selling.

If you have the "great American novel" that you've written sitting on your desk buried under rejection letters from publishing houses, the platform allows you to take advantage of an easy and low-cost way to get your book published and offer it for sale. If you have an idea for a book in your field of expertise, you can write your book or have it ghostwritten for you and publish on the KDP Platform. I call this Passion Project Books and success depends on how popular the field is, your ability to promote it and your writing skills. I will mention this here but there will be no accompanying chart as there are too many variables in this field. I do want frustrated authors and those with a message to share to know that this exists. You can accomplish a goal you have been passionate about with very little risk.

If you do not have the desire to write about your passion but still want to take advantage of the money-making opportunity for self-published books, you can write books in a series or in a specific category that are proven profitable niches. A Series is a collection of books that follow a character through different adventures, think Harry Potter.

Niche Books have a theme to them, such as "health" or "diet." The more popular the niche, the more competitive it will be to rank and sell your books, but you can really drill down to a specific subniche and find easier targets. In this instance you would research popular, but not yet saturated niches. Then, write or commission to have written books that you outline and get them ranked within that field. The key is a narrow focus within a popular niche.

For instance, In the "Diet" category, you'll find over 60,000 listings for books about the Keto diet. "Keto Diet for Women" cuts that number in half to 30,000. "Keto Diet for Women over 60" lowers that number tenfold to 3,000. Extensive research is required to locate a niche that is popular, but not overly popular, thus still competitive.

Once you have determined a viable niche, then you must write or hire a writer to create content that stands out in some way as to make you book more desirable than the others in the field. You can generate traffic to your book with proper keywords and category selection and you can use paid ads both on and off the Amazon platform to draw attention.

Many categories on Amazon are ripe for creating a Book Series. The upside of a series is that once one book becomes popular, readers will be clamoring to hear what happens next! Romance is one of the most popular categories of books on Amazon. Many authors create a series in this category. Some more broad, like "Harlequin Novels" which do not include the same characters from book to book but they do contain the same predictable formula that readers are drawn to over and over.

Other series are narrower in that they follow one or more characters through a series of adventures over several books. For this to succeed, one must choose a hyper targeted and super narrow niche. Permit me a silly example just to make the point: "Supernatural" Novels- too broad. "Vampire" Novel" - less broad. "Vampire Romance" Novels – getting narrower. "Lesbian Vampire Romance" Novels – narrow and very targeted.

There are tools and software that can help you identify potential niches. This model requires time to write or money to hire writers and extensive research as well as some ability to create or discern high-quality in the finished product.

While people on Amazon looking at books, are there to buy, you must still stand out among the thousands of other offerings. Besides paid ads, you could write (or commission) a captivating Press Release and pay a company to distribute the release, in the hopes of getting media attention to your book. You can also use some of the methods we discussed above for influencers: Getting booked as a podcast guest, writing blog posts for other content creators, engaging in forums where your target audience can be found or working with influencers.

**In order to be successful in the researched series/niche endeavor, you must:**

- Research popular yet unsaturated niches.
- Outline the book's characters and plot.
- Write or hire a writer to write the book.
- Design or commission a very compelling cover.
- Create multiple plots for future books in a series or multiple books within a specific niche.
- Drive traffic to that book through ads or word of mouth.
- Continue to develop new content for the next book in the series.

## Traffic Generation:

Awareness, Evaluation and Conversion: Shoppers on Amazon will already be searching within your niche for something to read, your work lies in the evaluation stage. Your books must stand out from other books within that niche. How difficult that will be depends on the niche you chose and the number of other competitors. Conversions are not an issue as Amazon is a trusted shopping source.

# BOOKS
## SELF-PUBLISHING

Degree of Difficulty to Learn — BEG

Upfront Costs — 0-($)

Time to First Sale — **2M-3M**

Income Potential

How Hard to Drive Traffic — **Medium**

Builds Your Email List — **Low**

Risk Level — **Low**

# LOW OR NO CONTENT BOOKS

If you don't have the skills or the desire to write an entire book, there is a whole subset of books known as low or no content. These books are easy to write or pay to have written. For this reason, this is an extremely competitive field on Amazon. Some examples of books that are low or no content include journals, coloring books and puzzle books. The most successful sellers in these types of books will niche down to a passionate audience.

For instance, offering a coloring book of "nature" is very broad but offering a coloring book of "Bible Stories for Kids" would allow you to advertise to a passionate subset of folks looking for very specific coloring books for their kids. Journal offerings are extensive and can be made in nearly every niche, Journal for Gardeners or Journal for Yoga Lovers would have tips and pictures throughout the lined pages aimed at the audiences of various niches (other journals for other niches could include recipes, crafting tips, inspirational quotes, etc.)

You can outsource the creation of all of these types of books to gig workers. Just type "Coloring Book maker" into Fiverr and you will see several listings of people willing to design a coloring book for $10-50. While this is a very easy type of selling to get into, it is a very crowded playing field. If you have a following already or have a very unique niche, there is still the opportunity to make money with low or no content books. Also, the cost of entry is low enough to test this method so you can test easily and see if your idea has legs.

You must decide on a niche initially, you can always branch out to other niches as you get some traction or if your first niche did not work out. If you want to make a journal, browse bookstores on and offline for "themed" journals and collect quotes, stories and pictures relevant to your theme. If you want to make a coloring book, create, or find in the public domain designs within your niche. Pay someone on Fiverr to turn those designs into a coloring book. Once you have the content generated and the graphics created, you list your book for sale and ... you guessed it, drive traffic to your listing. This can be done with paid ads both on and off the Amazon marketplace or with content creation to an audience you already have. If you have a series of these books, you could create a giveaway for the first in the series in order to spark interest in potential customers who would then be interested in more books in the series.

You could partner with a successful E-commerce seller in a similar niche and create a revenue sharing affiliate agreement. For instance, if a store owner offered Christian jewelry and apparel, you could approach that owner to help you market your Christian coloring books for kids.

The creation of these books is much simpler than the selling of these books and many who have found success in this field have several hundreds, even thousands of titles and have been in the space several years.

**In order to be successful in this endeavor, you must:**

- Research and Pick a Niche for your book.
- Design or commission a design for your book.
- Create an Amazon KDP Account.
- Upload that book to KDP and create a compelling optimized listing.
- Drive traffic to that book through ads, affiliates or word of mouth.

## Traffic Generation

Awareness, Evaluation and Conversion: Shoppers on Amazon may already be searching in your niche for a low content book or journal; your work lies in the evaluation stage. Your books must stand out from other books within that niche. How difficult that will be depends on the niche you chose and the number of other competitors. Conversions are not an issue as Amazon is a trusted shopping source.

# BOOKS
## LOW/NO CONENT BOOKS

Degree of Difficulty to Learn

BEG

Upfront Costs

$

Time to First Sale

**1M**

Income Potential

How Hard to Drive Traffic

Medium-High

Builds Your Email List

Low

Risk Level

Low

# BOOKS/PUBLIC DOMAIN PUBLISHING

Another way to make money online on the KDP Platform is to become a publisher. In a very simple way, you can learn by watching free videos on the amazon page itself or on YouTube about how to: format a manuscript, optimize the listing, write compelling descriptions and create compelling book covers. And then you can offer your publishing services to writers who need that service. This is more in the category of gig work though, and there is a better more lucrative way to create a business publishing on KDP. This is known as PUBLIC DOMAIN book publishing.

Many famous and popular books are no longer protected by copyrights. In the United States a work of art enters the public domain 70 years after the death of the author. In other countries, it varies from 50-80 years after death. So, very famous books like Dracula, Pride and Prejudice and War and Peace can all be published by anyone and sold on the Amazon Marketplace. These books can be found online through Project Gutenberg at gutenberg.org. According to their mission statement, the site was created to "encourage the creation and distribution of eBooks." The site now boasts 50,000 free books. The books are even listed in order of most often downloaded so you know what is popular at any given time. These books can be published as eBooks, paperbacks or hardcover books.

There is a KDP rule that if a book is available for FREE online, you are allowed to publish it on the marketplace, but you cannot charge for it since it is free and available online already. If you want to publish public domain eBooks, you must add to it in some way, either through illustrations or annotations, such as historical notes or both. Many illustrations are available in the public domain on other sites, so no need to be a talented artist.

While you must alter the eBook to publish on KDP, you do NOT need to alter the book at all to publish a paperback or a hardcover copy of these books. You simply download the html file, have it formatted to the specs KDP requires, create a book cover, and write and original description for the back cover. And, before you ask, the answer is yes, many people still buy paperback books, I promise.

This method of publishing books, once you learn how to do it properly, is one of the few true passive income opportunities online. Meaning, that once you put in the time and effort, and it does take an extraordinary amount of time and effort, the sales will continue to come in monthly without further effort on your part other than occasional maintenance of your library. Book cover creation, formatting and even book descriptions can be outsourced as well. The key to success in this business is volume and having your books stand out from the others by keywords, descriptions, and compelling book covers.

This is the Amazon Marketplace, so you are subject to their terms and policies which may change at any time. Initially, you will need to have a clear understanding of their requirements and do solid research into the issue of copyright based on the country and the author date of death.

**In order to be successful in this endeavor, you must:**

- Create an Amazon KDP Account.

- Familiarize yourself with copyright rules in the countries in which you intend to sell.

- Choose the book you want to download from Gutenberg and format it properly.

- Create a compelling eye-catching book cover so you stand out from the crowd.

- Write a unique description of the book to attract readers to your listing.

- Continue to publish these books regularly until you have enough sales to meet your monthly income goals, then you can slow down your production but still keep adding books and tweaking your listings if you see sales slipping.

## Traffic Generation

Awareness, Evaluation and Conversion: Shoppers on Amazon are already searching for your exact title, your work lies in the evaluation stage. Your books must stand out from other versions of that same book. How difficult that will be depends on the title you chose to publish and the number of other competitors. Conversions are not an issue as Amazon is a trusted shopping source.

# BOOKS
## PUBLIC DOMAIN BOOKS

Degree of Difficulty to Learn

BEG-INT

Upfront Costs

$$ $

Time to First Sale

**1M**

Income Potential

How Hard to Drive Traffic

**Low to Medium**

Builds Your Email List

**Low**

Risk Level

**Low**

# CHAPTER 6

# EXPERT TEACHER/ COURSE CREATOR

Just like in the real world, people who want to learn a new skill will seek out experts and courses online to gain the knowledge they are seeking. There are several ways that experts in certain fields can monetize their expertise. They can do one-on-one coaching, which is limited in scale as you are trading hours for dollars. They can do group coaching, teaching several students at once, which is more scalable, or they can create a course which is infinitely scalable as it exists as a series of videos and PDFs that can be distributed with a click of a button.

The more "touch points" you have with your students, the more you can charge someone to learn from you. For example, if the entire course is just a series of videos or a step-by-step book, the student will expect to pay a one-time fee, likely between $30 and $500. If you have a video series but also offer weekly live Q&A calls, then you can command more money because you are "teaching" them "in person." If you are working with small groups or one on one and offer daily access for a given time period, then you can command an even higher price. These are called "low ticket," medium ticket" and "high ticket" offerings. Very successful and lucrative businesses have been created with all of these "sharing your expertise" methods. The video series as a stand-alone offer relies on high volume of sales, but for certain fields, a video series maybe all anyone needs.

Let's look at an example of offerings a dog trainer might use to build a business. She could create a series of videos that teaches dog owners how to train a misbehaving dog. (Bonus: The trainer now has an email list of dog owners that he can offer his next video series to or products that he gets an affiliate commission for selling.) If she had the resources she could create a weekend retreat, where, for a much higher price, dog owners could bring their pets to her and receive one on one or small group instruction. She could create a group that you must pay to join wherein you would get daily or weekly lessons and be able to network with other pet owners. This is a create way to create what we spoke of earlier in the book, RMR, recurring monthly revenue. This is not an exhaustive list of what she could offer, but an example of different ways people are monetizing their expertise to make money online.

In the online world, any skill set can be monetized to some extent. You may not consider yourself an "Expert", but you don't need to have a PhD or some credentials to teach someone a skill you have that they do not. Knowing how to sew, or knit, how to bake or cook, how to train for a marathon make you an expert to someone who does not know how to do these things and is eager to learn. While certain skill sets involving health, wealth and relationships tend to be the most lucrative income producers, decent money can be made in any popular field.

A successful course or coaching program offers students step by step instruction or mentoring towards a specific outcome in a specific time period. The clearer you are on your offer, the better your course will turn out and the more success your students will have. You must create these steps and then decide on what platform you want to teach them: a video series, a membership site, a written series? Sites like Udemy.com will give you a sense of what skills others are teaching that you may not have imagined people would pay for, as well as show you how courses are organized. You are not limited at all to promoting on that site, I mention it for you to see offerings. Promotion should be multi-channeled for your best success.

Finally, once the course is created or the mentoring offer is perfected, you must...you guessed it, get traffic to that offer. Paid ads can target people in your desired audience and those folks can be enticed to join a list as discussed above with a free lead magnet, perhaps one step in your course in the form of a video or cheat sheet.

You can search for affiliates who will promote your course to their email list for a portion of the revenue. You can create your own online media presence and build up your own following with content creation that offers value before charging for a full-blown course. Once you have sold the course and had successful students, you can ask them for testimonials and ask for them to refer their friends to your course based on their own success. As throughout this book, there are various ways to get eyes on your offer but go into this type on online income knowing that this is a crucial step to success.

**In order to be successful in this endeavor, you must:**

- ♦ Identify your particular skill set.
- ♦ Create a step-by-step process to teach someone what you know from A to Z.
- ♦ Have a clearly designed goal that you promise students they will achieve in a specific time period.
- ♦ Create the course content or map out the live trainings you will offer.
- ♦ Decide on the platform you will use to house your offer
- ♦ Find people who want to learn what you are teaching.
- ♦ Continue to engage via email or groups with your students for future offerings, testimonials and referrals.

## Traffic Generation

Awareness, Evaluation and Conversion: You are responsible for all three stages of the customer's journey. You need to find the right buyers, make them aware of your offer and tell them about it in a way that is compelling enough, so they want to buy from you. Then you must have a website or course delivery system that appears trustworthy so they do not feel like they will be scammed or cheated.

# EXPERT / COACH
## COURSE CREATOR

Degree of Difficulty to Learn | BEG-INT

Upfront Costs | $ $

Time to First Sale | **2M-3M**

Income Potential

How Hard to Drive Traffic

**Medium to High**

Builds Your Email List

**High**

Risk Level

**Low**

# CONCLUSION

My goal is explaining these platforms in detail and rating the pros/cons and investments involved has been to open your eyes to a new world of possibility. I want you to see the whole picture that most other books, and few course creators provide. Creating an online profit stream takes work. The skills can be learned though, even by total beginners. Some platforms may take a little more time, others may take a little more money. You would be wise to invest in courses and software that can shorten your learning curve and speed up tedious manual procedures if you can afford to.

The questions I get asked the most from folks wanting to explore online income opportunities are answered below (listed alphabetically):

**In my opinion:**
**Which is Best for Total Beginners?**

◆ Affiliate Marketing

◆ Amazon Wholesale

◆ Course Creation

◆ Dropservicing/Agency

◆ Gig Work

◆ Public Domain Publishing

◆ Self-Publishing

## Which is the Fastest Way to Generate Income?

- ◆ Affiliate Marketing
- ◆ Amazon Wholesale
- ◆ DropServicing/Agency
- ◆ Gig Work

## Which has the Highest Income Potential?

- ◆ Amazon Private Label
- ◆ Amazon Wholesale
- ◆ Affiliate Marketing
- ◆ Branded E-Commerce Stores
- ◆ High Ticket Course Creation

I do not know all the secrets of success, but I do know the main one: You must get started. Choose the path you want to pursue. Find reliable mentors to help you on your path. Be willing to invest in yourself and in your future. Stay the course, even when things get hard. Your future self will thank you.

When I first started out online very few communities existed where one could go to get help. A few platforms had some level of support either free or paid as part of their offering, but they were not really geared to brand new sellers. Back then, I was shooting in the dark. I did not know what was really required in each platform and did not know any experts I could speak with to help decide which avenue to pursue. And once I chose a platform, I longed for someone I could check in with regularly to help with hurdles and roadblocks.

When I decided to dedicate my time and resources to helping people learn how to start their own online businesses, I thought a lot about what I would have wanted when I first started out. I remember feeling very alone and in over my head. I did not personally know anyone who was on my same journey. There were other people in courses I took who I saw on Facebook, but never a community of folks I felt I could confide in and get mentorship from. So, I recently set out to create a safe place where like-minded entrepreneurs at any stage of their journey could come and be mentored and inspired.

I wanted to create a mastermind community where folks could learn and grow together, holding each other accountable, celebrating each other's successes and encouraging one another when times get tough. I partnered with one of the most successful businessmen I know in the online marketing space, an 8-figure E-commerce seller who is as committed as I am to helping folks achieve financial freedom. Together we have found success in nearly every field discussed in this book. And now, we have created our own, very affordable, monthly Mastermind group, dedicated to helping people succeed online in any platform they choose, whether they are brand new, or have been in the game for years and are just stuck. If you want to explore how to create online streams of income without investing thousands of dollars upfront before you know what will work, then join us.

We will help you decide what the best opportunity is for you and once you choose a platform, we will be there to support you and answer your questions along the way. You will meet an incredible group of fellow entrepreneurs who are on the same journey as well.

Our Mastermind is called Create Profits Online. You can start a two-week free trial to see what it's all about by signing up here: https://onlineprofits.community. We offer bi-weekly live Q&A calls, courses, and trainings in how to find offers, how to choose between offers, how to generate traffic to your offer and how to build your email list. These skills, as you have read, will apply to any field you are considering. Further we have a DFY library of website and funnel templates and easy to copy emails sequences you can use for your own ventures on Day One. We also have a rolodex of vetted service providers to help you with tech issues if you want to outsource tasks to them. We are engaged in the community daily, answering questions and giving advice to keep you on track and get you unstuck. This book has given you the roadmap, our Mastermind provides the guided tour.

Whether you choose to join our community or find your own, remember to *keep moving forward*. Lots of things you excel at now you were new to you once. Don't' get discouraged by small setbacks. Stay the course. The reward is so worth the effort! I firmly believe that with hard work and the right mindset, success is inevitable. Cheers in advance to your success in creating an online stream of income!

# OVERALL COMPARISONS

| Platform | Difficulty Level To Learn | Upfront Costs | Time To First Sale | Income Potential | How Hard To Drive Traffic | Does It Build Your Email List | Risk Level |
|---|---|---|---|---|---|---|---|
| Amazon Private Label | INT-ADV | | 8m-12m | | Medium | Low-Medium | High |
| Amazon Wholesale | BEG | | 1m-2m | | Low | Low | Low |
| Amazon Merch | BEG | | 1m-2m | | Medium | Low | Low |
| DS Churn And Burn | BEG-INT | | 1m-2m | | High | High | Low |
| DS Branded Store | BEG-INT | | 2m-3m | | High | High | Med |
| Private Label Store | INT-ADV | | 8m-12m | | High | High | High |
| DS High Ticket | BEG-INT | | 2m-3m | | High | High | Low |
| DS Print On Demand Store | BEG | | 1m-3m | | High | High | Low |
| DS Subscription Box Store | BEG-INT | | 3m-6m | | High | High | Low |
| Affiliate Marketing Paid Ads | BEG | | 1m-3m | | Medium | High | Low |
| Affiliate Marketing Content Marketing | BEG | | 1m-3m | | Medium | High | Low |
| Affiliate Marketing Email Marketing | BEG | | 2m-4m | | Medium | High | Low |
| Affiliate Marketing Influencer | BEG | | 4m-8m | | Medium-High | Medium | Low |
| Gig Work | BEG | | 1m-2m | | Medium | Low | Low |
| Agency/Dropservicing | BEG | | 1m-2m | | Medium | Low | Low |
| Books Self Publishing | BEG-INT | | 4m-6m | | Medium | Low | Low |
| Books Low Or No Content | BEG | | 1m-2m | | Medium-High | Low | Low |
| Books Public Domain | BEG | | 1m-2m | | Low-Medium | Low | Low |
| Expert/Course Creator | BEG-INT | | 1m-3m | | Medium-High | High | Low |

**Degree of Difficulty:** How hard is for the average person to learn and implement this platform.

Is the platform good for:

*Beginners:* Folks completely new to the online money-making space.

*Intermediate:* Folks who have tried some online income opportunity with varying levels of success.

*Advanced:* Folks who have already had success making money online.

---

**Upfront Costs:** How much money do you need to begin. This cost analysis assumes that you will be paying for at least some education and/or software on top of what is required.

($) Under $1,000

($) ($) $1,000-3,000

($)($)($) $3,000-5,000

($)($)($)($) $5000-$10,000

($)($)($)($)($) Over $10,000

**Potential Income:** Average *monthly profit* for a successful seller, not a "dabbler" and not a "superstar."

💰 $500-$1K/month

💰💰 $1K-$5K/month

💰💰💰 $5K-$10K/month

💰💰💰💰 over $10K/month

---

**Generating Traffic to Your Offer:** How difficult will it be for you to get folks to see your offer. (Do not be dissuaded by a designation of high, with more effort generally comes more profit potential.)

Effort level:

*Low:* Fairly easy. Generally, means the platform has a traffic source already and standing out is not terribly hard.

*Medium:* Takes a fair amount of work or money for ads. For traffic to close a sale, you must stand out in a crowd of interested buyers where others are also competing heavily to stand out. For traffic to bring awareness to an offer and have someone else close the sale, you must generate that on your own, but that is not as difficult as generating buyer traffic.

*High:* Takes a lot of work or money for ads. You must create awareness for your own offers generate all the buyer traffic on your own.

**Own Your Own Customers:** Will this platform leave you with an Email List you own or a following online?

Likelihood:

*Low:* The platform is not set up for you to build your own customer list.

*Medium:* You can build a list with extra efforts, or you can build "followers" on a social media platform, but you must get their off-platform contact info yourself.

*High:* You build and own your list from the outset.

**Risk Factor:** What is the level of risk for you if you fail miserably. This mainly refers to monetary risk, not time spent.

Made in the USA
Columbia, SC
01 October 2022

68441618R00065